RIDE OUT THE STORM

Dr. Wanda Carr

NEW Publishing Company

Ride Out the Storm

No part of this book may be reprinted in any form without permission in writing from the publisher. All scriptures quotations were taken from the *Holy Bible*, King James Version.

Printed in the United States of America

© Copyright 2015 by Dr. Wanda Carr
All rights reserved.

ISBN-13:978-0692461778
ISBN-10:0692461779

carrwdc@hotmail.com

Table of Contents

1. Dedication — 4
2. Acknowledgment — 5
3. Foreword — 7
4. Introduction — 8
5. Storms of Life — 11
6. Don't Give Up — 23
7. P.U.S.H (Pray Until Something Happen) — 33
8. Delayed but Not Denied — 45

Dedication

I would like to dedicate this book to my daughter, Anassa Thompson. Baby you do not know how much it means to me the unfailing love you have shown me during your 21-years on this earth. Because of you I have fought through each storm with God's help to be that leading lady and mother that never put you in harm's way. The day of your conception, God knew you would be my biggest supporter and cheerleader. There were times I wanted to throw in the towel, but God had a way of using you to push me forward. I thank God for you every day and pray God will bless you as you mature into that beautiful flower he has called you to be. You are fearfully and wonderfully made.

Acknowledgments

I would like to take this opportunity to thank Dr. Bridget Newton for believing in me and encouraging me to write this book. Thanks to my editor/proofreader, Ms. Shirley Cox. I would like to thank my daughter, Anassa Thompson, my sisters and brothers, Debra Thompson, James Thompson, Marvin Thompson, Loura Thompson, LaToya Thompson, and John Thompson, III, especially my mother and father, John and Charity Thompson, for being supported of me and praying for me. I would like to thank my two nephews, DyQuan Bunns and Brandon Paul Thompson for providing me laughter and strength to endure this task.

I would like to thank my church family, St. Luke Pentecostal Healing Temple of Lewiston, NC under the leadership of our Interim Pastor, Bishop Michael Deloatch and First Lady Linda Gail Deloatch for their continuous prayers. I would also like to thank Pastor William S. Robinson and First Lady Patricia Robinson and the Holy

Temple Apostolic Church of Greenville, NC for keeping me lifted in prayer.

Finally, thanks to Arthur Clark of Clark's Photography, Leslie Bonds, and all of my family and friends that has supported me during the writing of this book. Your prayers and support are very much appreciated. Never could have made it without your prayers and support.

I pray that this book will bring healing and life to those storms that seems to overtake you.

FOREWORD

This book is a must have in the library of every believer as well as non-believers. Dr. Wanda writes with simplicity and enlightenment. This book touches you where you live. Dr. Wanda shares testimonies which are both inspirational and motivational. This book encourages you to praise God in spite of your circumstances. It produces healing that allows you to release praise. This book deals with reality. It meets you where you are in life. It addresses your heartaches, disappointments, failures, broken relationships and dreams that have been put on hold. God knew what we would go through in life and therefore gave us the tools we needed. This book also reveals that even though we may have plans for our lives, the ultimate plan, which is God's plan will prevail. It is never too late to fulfill your dreams. Through darkness and despair, there is hope. This book reminds us to stay focus, keep our eyes on Jesus and his promises. The Lord does have the last say in our lives. Dr. Wanda lets us know we are victorious in Jesus.

Shirley Cox

Introduction

Storms can appear in our lives in various forms such as: the death of a love one, divorce or separation, job loss, sickness, spiritual stagnation, etc. Whatever your storm may be, remember you have a storm chaser. Your storm chaser is Jesus Christ.

As I write this book, the devil has attacked me mentally and emotionally to give up on the completion of this book and life in general. I am happy to say I am still standing and it is by the grace of God. If the devil can attack our minds and get us to see it is no use, the devil knows he can have havoc with us. Dearly beloved, we are just doing life and the battle begins in our mind.

In reflecting back over the sermons God has allowed me to hear during this attack, I have been able to shed tears and continue to speak life over my situation regardless. Remember this one thing my friend "God wants to give you a crummy blessing" (Pastor Sheryl Brady); God wants to give you personal attention", and "Do not underestimate God" (Bishop Michael Deloatch). I am going one step farther do not underestimate God's power to turn that situation around. Greater things have yet to come. Greater things are still to be done.

We must remind ourselves daily; I must praise my way thru to get to where God promise me. Jeremiah 29:11 reinforces that God knows the plans he has for us. I never would have dream of writing a book nor doing the things I am doing now, if God did not used Pastor William S. Robinson and Dr. Bridget Newton to encourage me and speak life into me. I could not see myself praying in public/church or speaking in front of a congregation about my faith if Pastor Robinson did not take time to sow into my life. Thanks to Pastor Robinson, he has been working and developing those attributes by encouraging me to overcome those fears by doing, and now I do not feel uncomfortable praying in a public arena nor discussing my faith or ideas with others. Dr. Newton, believed that I could write a book, when I felt that it was not achievable, but what can I say, to God be the Glory for all the wonderful things he has done. God use them and others to push me into my destiny. We cannot see but we must trust God's guiding. In our going thru we must stay focus and remind the devil you cannot win this battle. We are human. Things will happen in our lives that can knock the very wind out of you. You may have to shed some tears, remember the shedding of tears is just to make your vision clear (Pastor Joey Baker).

I can attest to the devil ponding away at your emotions and feeding you negative thoughts about your situation. You can see everybody else being blessed and talking about how God made a way for them. My friend, continue to look up. Your day too will come. Trust God in all you do and he will see you thru. I pray as you read this book and continue to seek God during these troublesome times, that peace, and healing will overshadow you. God will give you a peace that surpasses all understanding. God will give you peace so during your waiting, you will be able to say Lord I thank you. I do not know when you are going to turn it around, how you going to turn it around, where you going to turn it around, all I know is I thank you for turning it around in my favor and working it out for my good.

Dr. Wanda Carr
Greenville, NC

Chapter 1

Storms of Life

Matthew 8:23-27 (ESV) And when he got into the boat, his disciples followed him. And behold, there arose a great storm on the sea, so that the boat was being swamped by the waves; but he was asleep. And they went and woke him, saying, "Save us, Lord; we are perishing." And he said to them, "Why are you afraid, O you of little faith?" Then he arose and rebuked the winds and the sea, and there was a great calm. And the men marveled, saying, "What sort of man is this, that even winds and sea obey him?"

Life can be so bitter. By the time you get out of one storm another storm is around the corner. In today's society, we are faced with so many uncertainties which, causes us to give up on life. I want to encourage you today that God wants to speak peace to your storm. You can hold your head up and begin to live again. It is not over until God says it is over.

We are constantly in the midst of storms. If you look around, there are storms everywhere. One thing we all know that Jesus is coming. And because of this, the devil is pulling out all of his weapons to destroy the bride. The bridegroom is ready to rapture the church away, but the church is not ready. We are living in perilous times that Paul talks about in II Timothy 3. There are wars and rumors of wars, fathers against sons, mothers against daughters, division in the church, and the economy is unstable. The storms of life are causing preachers, as well as the parishioners to commit suicide. I do not mean spiritual suicide, but taking their own lives because they do not know what to do. Men and women's hearts are failing them because the cares of this world has become overwhelming.

According to an article written in Crosswalk.com, by Kelly Givens (2013), Kelly pointed out some findings from Schaeffer Institute that 70 percent of pastors constantly fight depression, and 71 percent are burned out. If pastors are losing faith, how can we the followers have hope during these trying times? First of all we do have hope. Regardless of what is going on around us we must look to the hills from which cometh our help and strength (Psalm 121). David found himself in a lot of storms. Some of David's storms where caused by his own decisions, but if you read in the book of Psalms, David knew where his help came from and he always repented and praised God regardless.

Like David, we should find ourselves in constant praise and worship before God. The word lets us know not to be alarmed because the times we are currently living in will come. This is the beginning of many sorrows. I want to continue to remind you that Jesus is coming. Storms are raging all around us, but be reminded that the race is not given to the swift neither the battle to the strong, but to the one that endures to the end. Luke 21:26 lets us know that men's hearts will fail them because of fear. Fear comes from not knowing what to do during troublesome times. We must hold on and hold out during these times. We must study God's word and hide it in our hearts so that we can fight the devil. Our only weapon for fighting and winning is the Word of

God. If we do not study the word, we will find ourselves in the same situation as the disciples were while Jesus was asleep on the boat.

I am the first to say that the storms of this old world are not easy. I too have faced some major storms in life that caused me to want to give up. I am glad I had the body of Christ and my sisters and brothers in Christ to help me and keep me focused during those stormy times. On this day, March 18, 2015, I want to let you know that God has given me peace in the midst of my storm. The peace he has given me, you can have also, regardless of your situation. You may ask what storms have you faced? You seem to be successful and have a lot going for yourself. The secret is I do not look like what I have been through.

First, I had a baby out of wedlock at the age 21. I was married at the age of 22 and single again at the age of 25. I have been through bankruptcy, depression, a slight heart attack at the age of 40, attempted suicide, but God never left me. I have been rejected so much that I had almost lost hope. My spirit has been crushed by the church and people that I sought to please. Matthew 8, states, God only had to speak one word and things changed, PEACE.

The storms of life can cause us to give up all hope. We must stay encouraged and know that God can handle every storm that arises in our life. Life can deal you a bad hand. Remember, the hand you are dealt can change if you can only believe. Faith without hope does not change your situation. You must have the faith to believe, as well as, see your situation different from its current status.

My husband left me when I was 25 years of age. I could have felt sorry for myself and sung the blues. However, I took my energy and pursued a long time dream of obtaining an advanced degree. God allowed me to achieve all my dreams I had when I was a young girl. I wanted to be a teacher and have a professional career. I am now a professor at a university and have a professional career.

I had to read God's word daily to overcome my storm. It does not matter if you can't see your future, from God's view, your future looks brighter and bigger. God let us know in Psalm 84:11 that he will not withhold any good thing from us if we do what is right. Being a child of God has great benefits. Storms only come into our lives to make us into those chosen vessels God wants us to be. After the storm the sun always shines.

In looking at a storm on the natural side, the clouds get real dark, then there is thunder, rain, and wind depending on what type of storm is arising. After the thundering, lightning, wind, and rain, you can look out the window and see the sun peeping out and possibly a rainbow. This assures us that God is saying to us that if we can just hang in there, he will lighten our loads, put joy back in our lives, and put a smile on our faces, and peace in our hearts. We can count on God to do more for us than any other creature if we exercise our faith.

In exercising our faith, we must remember as the body of Christ, we are not exempt from the storms of life. The storms of life serve as a conduit for the miraculous power of God to be revealed to the body of Christ. In Biblical times, when the disciples were on the water, and the sea was raging, God asked the question "Why are ye afraid, o ye of little faith." Our faith has to be bigger than our circumstance.

I am reminded of some of the old martyrs in the Bible where their storms could have overtaken them. They could have lost all faith and hope. In the book of Job, we read Job lost everything he had. Job's body was afflicted with sores. Job knew that in the mist of it all, God was still in control. I would like to call on Hezekiah. In II Kings 20:1-2, Hezekiah was on his bed of affliction. The prophet Isaiah had a message from God to him. Hezekiah received the message to set his house in order, for he would die and not live. On Hezekiah dying bed, he turned his faced to the wall and prayed to God. God heard him and answered his prayer. You cannot tell me that God will not speak peace to your storm.

In God's eyes your storm is small. While reflecting over my life if I had fainted and given up each time a storm arose, I would not be here today. I will not tell you that it was easy, but with God's help, I was able to come out victorious. I can remember one instance where the devil tried to convince me to take my life. I am glad that I did not give in to those thoughts. Thoughts will come. There will be storms that come but we must hold on because David lets us know in Psalm 30:5, "Weeping may endure for a night but joy will come in the morning" (KJV).

You may be in a storm that is trying to overtake you. My child, if you can just visualize the process the trees endure during a storm. The trees bow, some are bent all the way down to the ground but when the wind stop blowing, and the storms cease, those trees stand tall again. It is mourning and weeping time now in your life, but you will stand tall again. I am glad to report that I am standing tall today. I do not look like what I have been through.

    I could have or should have lost my mind when my husband walked out, or when I had a baby out of wedlock at the age of 21. I could have or should have been dead when I was playing with a gun and pointed it to my head and did not know it was loaded and cocked ready to fire. God looked out for me. I could have or should have been sitting in a homeless shelter because I lost everything at one point in my life. God kept me here for such a time as this. You too may have the same testimony. Reflect back over your life and look how far God has brought you. Can't you see the storms did not overtake you? Hallelujah anyhow! The devil thought he had you but you got away. If God brought you through that storm do you not believe he will continue to carry you through? My friend stay encouraged and be strong; your help is on the way. This is a season of breakthrough. Your latter will be greater than your former.

Prayer

God the storms of my life is more than I can handle. I need your renewed strength to help me get through these storms. Lord prepare me for what is about to take place in these last days. Do not let the storms cause me to turn and deny you. Give me the strength to endure and see your face in peace. God I know I can only find peace with you because I have no one else to turn to. God cover my family and my friends so we can be helpers one to another during our difficult times. Jesus I need you. You are my Lord, my God, and my King. You are worthy of all of my worship and praise. Help me to know you and love you so deeply and dearly that the storms of this old world will fade away and grow strangely dim. I know you are working on my behalf. I need your power, your grace, and your love so that no matter what life brings my way, I can respond to each situation the way you would respond. It is all for your glory. I do not want to respond outwardly but rather from within, from the river of living waters. May I find all of my joy in you. Amen

Chapter 2

Don't Give Up

Acts 27:1-44 (KJV) But the centurion, willing to save Paul, kept them from their purpose; and commanded that they which could swim should cast themselves first into the sea, and get to land: And the rest, some on boards, and some on broken pieces of the ship. And so it came to pass, that they escaped all safe to land.

After all you have been through you cannot give up. In Acts 27, Paul was a prisoner headed to Rome and a storm occurred. In verse 10, Paul had received a revelation from God that the voyage would not be successful and lives could possibly be lost. I believe God was speaking to Paul concerning the safety of the voyage, but the passengers chose to disregard his warning. Like today, people are still turning a deaf ear to the voice of God and instead of listening to him they have chosen to follow their own course and abide by their agenda.

When the storms begin raging uncontrollably, Paul said to the centurion and to the soldiers, except these abide in the ship, ye cannot be saved. The verses that really bless my soul are verses 42-44, when the centurion wanting to save Paul, commanded that they which could swim should cast themselves first into the sea, and get to land. The last verse is the key verse of this scripture, some made it on boards, and some on broken pieces of the ship. We must remember, sometimes in life we have to rely on the broken pieces to get us to our destination.

A broken piece can represent anything in your life. It can be an addiction, prostitution, lying, stealing, cheating, gangs, sexual immorality, or whatever the devil has placed in your life to hinder your relationship with God. But I want to admonish you not to give up. But hold fast to the word of God that is able to destroy every yoke of bondage in your life. I know for certainty, you can make it on broken pieces. Your darkest hour is just before dawn.

You may be sick in your body, and about to give up on your healing; but I declare to you what you are going through is not going to take you out. What God has spoken over your life shall come to pass. For those of you who may be asking the question, what about those that were sick and did not receive their healing on this side? Remember, God knows what is best and never makes any mistakes. As long as they died in faith like the martyrs of old, they have a brand new building not made by hands, no more sickness, disappointment, heartaches, and pain, no more suffering, because they will be with Jesus. Where Jesus is there is peace and joy forever more. Where Jesus is, you can walk around heaven where there is no sickness and the streets are paved with gold. You will be able to sing a song the angels cannot sing. I have been redeemed, washed by the blood of the Lamb. Revelation 22 tells us of the trees that are in the midst of the garden were we will be able to feast on the leaves for the healing of the nations. Wow, what a day that will be.

We cannot give up. As God begin to deal with me about riding out the storm, I begin to look around and ask God about the storms we are in. God began to speak to me, he said, take a look at the economy, look at families and marriages, and look at the body of Christ. There are rumors of wars, the economy is financially unstable, lack of job security, satanic attacks on families and marriages. The divorce rate is extremely high within the body of Christ. Division and competition has filled our sanctuaries. We as a people have moved so far away from our Christian values, but Christians and others that use the Bible as their road map can rest assured there is light at the end of the tunnel if they just hang in there.

    The body of Christ must set a high standard when it comes to how we represent and present Christ to those that are lost. We cannot be the salt of the earth that is mentioned in Matthew 5:13, if when we are faced with adversity, we faint. We must show the world the strength and power of God during our storms. How will the sinner have faith and hope that there is a brighter day if the body of Christ has given up? In James 1 verses 1-12, he reminds us to count it all joy when we are faced with divers trials. We have to praise God through our storms. Storms are only temporary.

Do not give up on what God has spoken in his word concerning your storms and how he is going to bring you out.

In our eyes, it seems as though we are not coming out, but in God's eyes we have already won the battle and have the victory. Victory comes in all forms. I have not been working full-time for the past 3-years. I have prayed every day asking God to bless me with a full-time position with benefits. As of today, I have been employed with the same Temporary Agency for the past 2 years. I have applied and interviewed for jobs within the company and outside of the company. I have applied to Temporary Services and marketing myself to gain employment. But nothing has manifested. This has been an ongoing storm in my life. God has been speaking to me since 2013 to this present time about the blessings that are preparing to take place in my life.

Despite my present situation, God has allowed me to pay my vehicle off, purchase a vehicle for my daughter, complete and graduate with another masters' degree, and travel on a minimum income. God constantly reminds me that provision does not come from the job, money or the education I have achieved; but provision comes from him. I still am pursuing full-time employment, but my prayer now is God what is your will for me? God has used people to prophetically speak blessings and favors in my life. Recently, I received a call from my prayer warrior and mentor, she told me that God said "He has me right where he wants me to be and when he gets ready to move me it will be to the place that he has specifically designed for my life in this hour." One would think I would continue to rejoice and be glad that God is answering my prayers. But even though God is continuing to prove himself on my behalf, the devil still tries to keep my spirit a little unsettled. The Lord spoke through my pastor one Sunday that he heard my petition and all I had to do is just praise him, but the devil still wants me to be uneasy.

Today, I believe what God has spoken. I pray daily Lord help my unbelief. I have to believe and see it in my spirit that what he has spoken is being manifested. I might not see it with my natural eye, but I believe it is on its way. We all have prayer requests before God. We have been petitioning him about those storms that are currently in our lives, but still there is no answer. You know that you should have lost everything. Your bills should have not been paid, but God! Can I say but God did not let it be so? All God have to do is speak one word to our storms and circumstances will change. However, we can delay and prolong our change when we try to fix things and figure things out. Stop trying to figure things out and let God work them out.

I cannot explain to you how I made it over. All I can tell you is that God brought me through. It was no goodness of my own but his grace and mercy provided me with guidance during my storm. The storms are still raging in my life but I am reminded of a song by Douglas Miller written some years ago. The song says, though the storms keeps on raging in my life and sometimes it is hard to tell the night from day. My soul has been anchored in the Lord. As long as you have been anchored in the Lord you will arrive on shore safely. Our hope must continue to stay in Jesus. There is no other way out of the storm but through the grace and mercy of Jesus Christ.

I would like for you to let your mind wander for a little while. Think about you sitting on the bay watching the boat that has been anchored or tied down after the fishermen has come back to shore. The boat does not look like the storms it had to endure during the fishermen trip. However, the boat has been anchored anticipating its owner to go back out to sea. That is just like God. The storms in our lives can be so severe that we almost capsize. God sits high and looks low and calms the raging seas so we can catch our breath and go further. Once we catch our breath, there is another storm that arises and we have to take a deep breath and go back to battle.

My friend be encouraged. The storms are going to get better. We must rest and trust that God will see us through. God lets us know in Proverbs that we are to trust him and not lean to our own understanding but acknowledge him and he will direct our paths. When you trust God, you do not have to sit up all night and babysit your storm. You can give it to him and he will handle it. God does not slumber nor sleep and he is the storm chaser. When God chases the storm away it is done well.

There is an old hymn that says "there's a storm out on the ocean and it is moving this old way. If your soul is not anchored in Jesus you will surely drift away." We do not want to drift away when our storms arise. If you feel you are about to go under, I encourage you to pray the following prayer:

Prayer

Dear Heavenly Father. I do not know what to do or how to handle this situation I am currently in. You told me I could cast all my cares on you because you careth for me (I Peter 5:7). I believe and have the faith to know you are concern, because if you were not, I would have fainted a long time ago. The storms of life have almost drained the life from me. I ask you dear Master to give me renewed strength to endure this storm. I know that this storm will pass and the sun will shine again. I know I am victorious because you have already fought my battle. I believe you are working on my behalf. I declare and decree this storm to cease in Jesus name I pray. Amen.

Chapter 3

P. U. S. H (Pray Until Something Happens)

Acts 16:25-34 (KJV) And at midnight Paul and Silas prayed, and sang praises unto God: and the prisoners heard them. And suddenly there was a great earthquake, so that the foundations of the prison were shaken: and immediately all the doors were opened, and every one's bands were loosed.

In every storm there is a waiting process. On the natural side we have to wait until the storm passes. After each storm there can be a catastrophe. There is a clean-up that takes place and things begin to get back in order. Things are never the same, but we are able to get our lives organized. Think for one moment, is that not how the storms of life leave us? We can go through so much in a lifetime, but in the end we win the battle. We are victorious. We must stop being the victim and start speaking victory over our lives. You have the victory through Jesus Christ our Lord.

When Jesus died on that cross and rose on Easter morning, he got up with all power. We have to P.U.S.H.

(Pray Until Something Happens). Do you think Paul and Silas were in the prison talking and twiddling their fingers saying, Oh we are in prison, nobody cares about us, and Lord why us? No, Paul and Silas prayed and a jail house rock took place. God wants to rock your situation right now. Go down on your knees in prayer and tell your problems to God. When you get up, get up in faith and with a praise in your mouth. Remember your praise is your weapon.

God told Jehoshaphat in II Chronicles 20:15, that the battle is not his but the Lord. Sometimes we just have to show up. God has already fought the battle and you won. How did you win? We win through the grace of God. God fights our battles. Why you are trying to figure it out? God have already worked it out. In thinking about the Israelites, as they walked around the wall of Jericho, they praised God. In their praise did the walls not come tumbling down?

There are times in our lives we have to bow our heads, say a prayer, and weather the storm. In weathering the storm, we are overcomers. In I Thessalonians 5:16-18, the word tells us to rejoice, pray without ceasing, and in everything give thanks for this is the will of God through Christ Jesus concerning you. We must continue our relationship through prayer. Prayer is the only way we can make it through our storms.

In my reading, I ran across this reading and it made me begin to rethink my storms. When a train goes through a tunnel and it gets dark, you do not throw away the ticket and jump off. You sit still and trust the engineer to get you through the dark place into the light. Likewise, you must trust God today no matter how dark your situation. God says, "You are coming out!" All I can say is wow! Powerful! In our storms we cannot jump overboard. We must stay in the ship until the storms cease and trust God to make everything alright.

As I write this book, the devil has come against me in the completion of this project. In my attack, I had to pray, mediate, and ask my prayer warriors to pray that God will remove the writer's block, so I can finish what God has birthed within me. We are living in a time where everything is so fast paced that our minds are constantly racing. When the devil attacks our minds he knows he has won the battle. We must purpose in our hearts to allow our minds to rest so that God can deal with us. In the mind is where our creativity begins. The mind is where God birth new ideas into our spirits. If we can think it, God can manifest the thought. Our thoughts are powerful. If you can dream it and imagine it, it is possible. Luke 18:27 clearly says "What is impossible with man is possible with God. People can tell you all day long it is not achievable, but remember if God furnished you with the dream, vision, and creativity, he will perfect it.

Saints we have to Pray Until Something Happens. I am reminded of our fore parents. They were born into slavery and did not have very much. They banded together through prayer and helping one another to accomplish a lot of things. Today, we are reaping the benefits of their prayers. They were being beaten, they were told no, they had to give up their seats, but I believe now we can go anywhere in the world we desire and enjoy the life we imagine. Saints we must continue in our faith. We must fight on and stay united. Let us think on the words of Dr. Martin Luther Kings' speech "I have a Dream". In Dr. Kings' dream, God allowed him to visualize how the world should look and how we should be united with one another and not divided by prejudices that come to separate us from being a unified people. We must continue to pray for each other and the spirit of love and unity amongst each other. We too, must continue to dream of a better place and better life for everyone.

We must get up every day and purpose in our hearts, mind, body, and soul that I will no longer be the victim. Tell yourself no matter how bad it is or how bad it gets; I'm going to make it!!!! We can make it if we try. The martyrs in Bible times had the right to give up; but they knew that God was able to bring them out of whatever situation they were in. I have heard people say, "well the preacher keeps telling me it is going to get better", "hang in there God is going to answer your prayers", "baby don't go back", "your blessing is on the way". Well like you, I have said why I have not received my blessings? You have a man; I am still single. You have the good job and I am still searching. You are a millionaire; you do not have to worry about anything. I have been praying and waiting just like you, but I have not gotten any release. I want to encourage you, my sisters and brothers to hang in there. Why should you hang in there? First of all, if God did it for them he will do the same for you. You must keep the faith.

My mother told me one day, in my talking to her, about my frustration about why no one would offer me a permanent job. My mother's comment was because I had wavering faith. She told me God is not going to work with wavering faith. I would say, my faith is not wavering. I have faith. I believe and trust Gods' word. What I did not realize was when I got by myself; I would second guess Gods' promises to me. I would have faith and believe God would work the impossible on my behalf. When I did not see it in a certain timeframe I would become disheartened and began to say God is not answering my prayers. Well, that was unwavering faith. When I was around others I would encourage them and have a spiritual high as if God had already answered my prayers. As the rejection letters arrived I would say, God I did everything you asked me to do why didn't you give me that position? I was qualified and met all the job qualifications.

The Lord let me see, that it is not what I want for you. I have something bigger and better. As of today I still have not received the permanent position, but I have become at peace within myself knowing God is working on my behalf. I asked God to remove any doubt and help my unbelief. The word of God lets me know that I only have to have faith the size of a mustard seed. A mustard seed is very small. We all have a measure of faith. This not only goes to the Christians, but this goes to the non-believers. God lets us know in Matthew 5:45 that he rain on the just and on the unjust. The unjust is not exempt from being blessed or reaping the benefits of Gods' promises. God says in II Peter 3:9 that his desire is that no one should perish, but that we all come to repentance. God is not going to force us to serve him.

    Praying is our only way of communicating to our Heavenly Father. There are angels assigned to each of us. If we do not pray to God, he cannot dispatch angels to work on our behalf. There is an old hymn that says

"Saints don't stop praying for the Lord is nigh. Don't stop praying he will hear your cry. The Lord has promised and his word is true. Don't stop praying he will answer you". The devil knows if he can get us to stop praying he can play with our minds. Joyce Meyers has a book out that says "Battlefield of the Mind". I pray and mediate daily, Lord Help me to think on those things you have promised me. We have to study our Bibles. If you do not feed yourself with the right words, when the devil attack, you have nothing to fight with. The Bible is our weapon. The warfare and fight on hand is not something we should take for granted. We are not wrestling with flesh and blood, but against the principalities, against the powers, against the world-rulers of darkness (Ephesians 6:12). In fighting against such powers, constant prayer is our only weapon.

When the devil brings up negative thoughts, you must use the word of God to defeat him. If the devil tell you, your sickness is until death, you must tell that devil he is a liar because Isaiah 53:5 says he was wounded for our transgressions, he was bruised for our iniquities, the chastisements of our peace was upon him; and with his stripes I am healed. You have to make it personal. When he tell you that you not going to get married, you have to quote Genesis 2:18, the Lord God said, it is not good that man should be alone. Did he not make Adam a helpmate when he was in the garden? Young ladies and gentlemen while we are waiting on our mates, we must remind ourselves of the scriptures that pertain to us as we wait. God said his word will not return to him void. If God said it, you have to believe it. God is not like man, he cannot lie. The failure is not in God but in us. Why? We stop praying, when we do not see results. We cannot stop praying when we do not see results. We must continue to pray and seek God for his will for our lives.

Prayer

God I pray for my sisters and my brothers that are waiting on you to answer their prayers. You said in your word that we can come boldly to the throne of grace. When we come to the throne of grace you told us in your word that is where we can find mercy and find grace to help us in the time of need (Hebrews 4:16). There are some single brothers and sisters that have been praying for their mates and still have not found that mate. Lord, I ask you to encourage their faith. Give them the strength to endure and continue to seek you. In their waiting process, Lord, give them a peace in their spirit that they will not yield to temptation or pursue the wrong mate. Lord, I know you cannot, will not, and shall not lie. I speak life over my sisters and my brothers. Lord, give them a fresh wind and let them realize they too can continue on in ministry until you reveal your perfect will. Lord I pray for that single mother or father raising their children alone. Lord, provide resources and whatever they need to endure the storm of raising their children to respect your Holy word.

God, I ask you to make a way for those individuals that are seeking employment and promotions. You said promotion does not come from the east, nor the west, nor from the south, but from you alone (Psalm 75:6). God I know you are a prayer answering God. You may not come when we want you but you are always on time. Lord, we do not understand all that you are doing, but God; we are going to use our mustard seed faith to continue to trust that you know what is best for us. You said you will perfect those things that concern us. God, I know you are concerned about us. You know about all of our needs, our wants, and our heart desires. God we commit them unto you. God have your way in our lives. Do what you want to do as long as you want. God we believe it and it is done in Jesus name we pray. Amen.

Chapter 4
Delayed but Not Denied

Some of you have been praying and petitioning God daily to speak peace to your storm. There are prayers that you have lying on the altar and they have been there for some years. Saints we have to remember our prayers can be delayed but not denied. I am reminded of Daniel 10:12 where the angel of God told Daniel to fear not, Daniel; for from the first day that thou didst set thine heart to understand and to chasten thyself before thy God, thy words were heard, and I am come for thy words. Daniel prayed, but he did not receive his answer. But I am here to declare that it only takes one word from God to answer your prayers. For 21 days, if you read the chapter, Daniel's prayer was held up. But Daniel still continues to petition God.

We have to continue to pray even when we do not receive an answer. I can relate to how some of you feel. I have said many times, Lord when will it be my time?

God I am trying to live to the best of my ability. I believe in what your word says, but God I still do not understand why my prayers have not been answered. I can encourage and pray for others to receive blessings but for some reason I cannot get a grasp of believing God can and will work the impossible for me. I am here to encourage someone. Continue in the faith, do not give up. As I encourage you, I am encouraging myself that my prayers may be delayed but they are not denied.

Sometimes we feel we are ready for the blessings we are praying for, but because God is omniscient and knows all things, he knows that we are not mentally capable of handling what we are asking for. If God chose to bless some of us with the things we have been praying for, we may never pray again. We might become consumed by the spirit of pride. Some things are in our lives to keep us on our knees and to keep us in remembrance of God provisions. We must not think that we are sufficient based on our knowledge, abilities or our accomplishments. All blessings and accomplishments come from God. He takes pride in our achievements but he does not want them to define who we are and to take the place of who he is in our lives.

As we look around us, we must recognize there is nothing stable. The only stability we have is in Jesus Christ. We must stay in continuous prayer like the disciples did for Peter. We must continue to remember our prayers can be delayed but not denied. God does not deny his children, but he wants to see if we are willing to wait until he decides to give us what he wants us to have. If God was an unjust God, do you think he would wake you up each morning? Every morning you rise, it is a new day filled with grace and mercy. What you did on yesterday has been erased and thrown into the sea of forgetfulness. We hinder ourselves when we allow yesterday's mistakes to control our future.

God can give us an answer to our problem, and because he does not respond in the way we anticipated, we feel as though he has not fixed our situation. God works things out according to the counsel of his own will. The ultimate goal is that he receive glory in our circumstances. Some of us are delaying our own destiny not because of our personal issues but because we are not willing to release others. You cannot walk in complete deliverance until you are willing to forgive yourself and others. Today, begin to free yourself from the people and things in your life.

When you encounter the peace and joy of knowing that your God can do anything, you can burst through the doors and say, "There is nothing today that God and I cannot accomplish". Father, even though I cannot see your hand. I know you are working on my behalf. God wants us to know that the delay is only because he is working something in us or working something out of us. God does not want you to become dependent on the blessings and forget about the one that blesses you.

Storms are in our lives to make us stronger. When a farmer plants a seed, he does not go out to the field every day to watch what he planted. He plants it and goes about his or her daily occupations. Finally, one day the farmer starts to see his crops coming up out of the ground. This is how we should treat our storms. When we take them to the throne of grace, leave them there. Thank and praise God in advance for working it out. It may take 30-years before the storm cease, but remember, delays don't mean denial.

Denial means it will never happen. God did not tell you he was not going to work on your behalf. He said he would work it out in his time, therefore we must faint not. Saints let us stop fainting along the way. When a runner runs a marathon, the runner's breathing changes; the runner becomes exhausted, the runner desires water, but does the runner stop in the middle of the marathon because of these conditions? NO! The runner is reminded of the training he has taken on before he started the competition. He thinks about his trainers' words of encouragement along the way. You are almost at the finished line. Do not give up. You are almost there. You have prepared for this day. The race is not given to the swift nor the battle to the strong but to him that endures to the end. (Ecclesiastes 9:11). You can only be denied something when you lose hope. When you yield to the negative and naysayers, and lose focus then your prayer is denied. Hold on my sisters and my brothers, failure is not an option in this walk of life. You may fall down but quickly get back up. When you get back up dust yourself off and begin to fight again. You lose when you throw up your hands and walk away. God has already fixed the fight to turn out in your favor.

Are you in the land of the living? Can you breathe in and out this morning? Can you see your family? Guess what? You are blessed. You may not have everything you want, but who does? The rich man may have all the money but guess what, he has to be concerned about people wanting to be his friend. Sickness does not have any respect of person. Just like you can become sick, the rich man can suffer likewise. He may be able to pay for all the materials things he wants, but he can't buy his healing.

We must not measure or judge ourselves based on others. Your storm can change immediately when God becomes your focus. Focus means to worship and praise God not because you have the answer, but because you are secure in knowing that there is no failure in God. I heard a preacher say "I am one thought away from my next miracle". When you are one thought away from your miracle, it means your miracle is in view. The devil will slip his crooked foot in to make us get off course if we chose to listen to him.

I want to let you know that everything you have been through is not wasted. God can use your delays to be a set up for where he is taking you. When God is taking you to another level, everybody cannot ride with you. If you read in the Old and New Testament, you notice that every time God was about to do something big, the individual had to separate from amongst their kindred. In the book of Genesis, God instructed Abraham to leave his kindred. Moses when he saw the burning bush God spoke to him in regards to his destiny and the work he had for him. Your destiny is birthed out of the storm, but you must continue to fight until God delivers. God cannot get our attention when there are other distractions. God can place storms in our lives to challenge and push us forward to our destiny and purpose.

If God allows you to encounter a storm, remember wherever you are, God is there with you. God told Moses he was standing on Holy ground and to take off his shoes. You may not actually see a burning bush, but God is calling you in prayer through your storm. Your storm will birth out an authentic praise within you. Praise instead of complaining as you go through your storms. God has to take some of us through storms to gain experience and discipline in order to have creditability to lead others. Your creditability will be your testimony to others of how God made provision for you during your struggles.

I can use my experiences, my sufferings, and storms as a testimony to encourage other single, professional women. My testimony of going through bankruptcy yet enabling me to purchase a car in the midst of it can be a testimony to someone in a financial dilemma. There was a time in my life when I was ashamed to invite people to my home because of my living conditions. I declare today that God will turn it around and let you build your own home. All is not lost. Your prayers will be answered in Gods' timing. There was one point in my life I wanted a nice car like others, but I had to ride around in a car that was not considered sporty. People would say, you are driving an old woman's car (Plymouth Acclaim). There were times I would cry, Lord when will it be my time? God blessed me with a job wherein my first paycheck was $1900. I was so excited I went to the car dealership the same day and purchased a car. I was able to put $500 cash down on a 2000 Toyota Camry and drove off with my blessing. God continued to bless me to make other purchases.

When I purchased my home, the Lord had an individual in my life to get me in position to receive my blessing. She instructed me to go out and scout the land and see what God had waiting for me. I remembered how the realtor showed me several different properties, the home I was looking at needed some repairs. The realtor made the comment why would you ride in a Volkswagen when you can ride in a Cadillac. In other words, why would I purchase a house and have to fix it up, when there were some land available? I could build and design the home the way I desired. June 2015 will be my 10-year anniversary of being a homeowner. I was single, did not have a man in my life, and was not receiving any assistance from my daughter's father. God provided for me. The Lord allowed the city in which I lived to pay off half of the house with my signing a contract that I will stay in the house for 10 years. After my 10 years, I can sell the house at the appraisal price and not have to give them any of the funds. Don't tell me God will not provide for his children.

In 2013, God spoke to me to resign from a position that I believed he had given to me. I prayed and questioned God. I was torn between leaving the job and staying. God spoke and told me that I have a ram in the bush, trust me. I have been without full time employment since 2013, but God has not let me down. God allowed me to hear about a federal government program that would pay my mortgage until 2016. God has opened doors that man thought were closed in my face. God has been sending and providing finances to allow me to pay my bills on time. I have not lost anything. The ram I was expecting was this big time job, paying six figures. God had another agenda in mind. The ram in the bush was to increase my faith and to get me to depend on him and not a job, an individual or my bank account. I thank God for all the provision he has provided for me.

My mentor reminds me that you are a Joseph. I did not understand at first, but now I know what she meant. When Joseph was in prison, he was able to interpret the dreams of the butler and the baker. When the butler was restored back to his rightful place, Joseph asked him to remember him. The butler forgot about Joseph, but when Pharaoh had his dream, the butler remembers Joseph, and Joseph was placed over all of Pharaoh's belongings (Genesis 40). Remember, nothing you have been through will be wasted. God uses everything to teach us a lesson. We must use those stormy parts of our lives to be testimonies to others. When God brings you from the dungeon to the presence of the king, you will be trained and know how to handle yourself in any given situation. God will instruct and teach us how to serve others without being lifted in pride. We will have the confidence that God will work on our behalf. God will put you in a wilderness and in a desert place to show you how great and mighty he is. God can take those things that are simple to teach us how to become great as we experience our storms.

Survival mode is what God is teaching us when we are going through our storms. Storms will become more intensified as end times draws nearer. The end times will push us into trusting God. The word lets us know that the just shall live by their faith. How can you say you are living by faith if there are no needs in your life? If you are never experiencing some type of storm, how can you be a witness to the peace of God to someone else? Without storms you don't have a testimony. You cannot lead or bring people to a place of deliverance if you both are in the same state. Someone must have the experience to lead those that feel they have no hope. If you never seen God work a miracle or have given you a breakthrough, you can only talk about others experiences. God does not just want you to talk about what he has done for others or in Biblical times, God wants you to tell the world what he has done for you. God wants to make sure when he put you in a place you are equipped to handle whatever he brings into your destiny.

I am getting happy in my spirit; because I believe that some of you are just waiting for one word to push you into your destiny. Your storm can become a place of blessings if you can understand what God is doing. If you can only think on the goodness of Jesus and all he has already done for you, you should be crying out in your soul, Hallelujah! I thank God for saving me. The accident that could have taken your life, the bullet that did not have a name on it could have destroyed you and your family, the tornado that claimed lives and homes all around you, but God! Even if you have undergone negative circumstances such as experiencing being hurt in an accident, losing a loved one to a bullet, or experiencing major loss during a tornado, but you can still say I am still standing.

We have to understand, earthly things do not mean anything without Jesus. No one has ever been to a funeral and seen a U-Haul hooked to a hearse. Some of our prayers and storms are because we are trying to be like the Joneses. I want to let you know, if you are trying to be like somebody else then you are living for all the wrong reasons.

Begin to seek God for those things that he wants you to have and do to build the kingdom of God. We all have a different purpose. Your purpose is not like my purpose. What is your passion? Remember, God is in the business of working miracles. What is that one miracle you want that you do not have a hidden agenda? When we go in prayer with hidden motives and agendas God is not moved. God is not moved by our big words. If you can only say help or have mercy, God will move just as quickly as he did for those individuals that prayed in Biblical times. We do not have to pray like the Pharisees, but instead be like the tax collector in Luke 18:9-14 who asked the Lord to have mercy on him because he was a sinner.

Praying is a two way conversation. Sometimes in your prayer time, pray and take a moment to listen to see what God has to say to you. Sometimes you might get down on your knees and you may not have any words to say. I just want to encourage you today when you can't find words to say, just say God, I thank you. Your thank you praise can be for anything.

The saints of old use to say, sometimes you have to pray in a manner that the devil becomes confused. There are sometimes you have to speak into the atmosphere and speak things into existence. God understand us when we use few words or many words. It is not how many words we can say, but it is the sincerity of the prayer. Sometimes I just pray in my spirit or out loud and say HELP ME LORD! Sometimes, I have prayed, I have petitioned, I have written down all my prayer requests, I have asked others to pray for me and pray with me. There is still no result. In my spirit I say, HELP ME LORD! There will be times in your life you do not know which direction to take. This is when your prayers become one word or a mourn. When you mourn or cry you may not understand, but God sees and knows all things. There is nothing that happens around you and to you that is unknown to God.

Prayer time should not be just a time for us to ask for things and more things. Prayer time should be a time of thanksgiving, humility, and praying for others. What you make happen for others God will make happen for you. Stop praying only for yourself and your four, but learn how to pray for others. You must be concerned about others that are going through storms. I was talking to some friends, and as they were talking I realized, my storm was nothing compared to what they were going through. They have a full time job and are struggling to make ends meet and I have a Temp job and God is opening and making provision for me and I still want to complain. I recognized after talking to those individuals, what I have can be what I had if I do not stop complaining.

When I am able to dine out I say thank you Lord for the meal. When I walk in my house and my lights are still on, I find myself telling the Lord thank you. My nephew (DyQuan) told me one day, Aunt Wanda you will go to shouting anywhere when God does something for you. I believe in giving him praise. I do not mean give him praise in public whereas you will be escorted out of a place of business. There is a way to thank God for what he has done for you.

God is not about big things. The woman in Mark 12:42 gave two small copper coins, which were worth less than a penny, but God called his disciples and told them this poor widow has put in more than all the contributors to the treasury. What you think is little; God looks at it as being much. Do not compare, measure, or size yourself with others. Be yourself and let God do the measuring. When you come out of your storm, you will be like pure **<u>Gold</u>**!!

Author Bio

Dr. Wanda Carr, is the owner/operator of Helping Hands Consultant, a consulting firm located in Greenville NC, specializing in tax preparation, accounting, mentoring and coaching services.

Dr. Wanda holds an AAS in Information System Technology from Martin Community College; BS in Business Administration/Management from Shaw University, a MBA in Business Administration, a MSA in Accounting all from Liberty University, and a DBA in Business Administration from Argosy University.

Dr. Wanda has a passion for teaching, mentoring and coaching others. Dr. Wanda continues to seek ways to research and study the progression of women in the 21st century, and ways to motivate, encourage, and empower individuals.

Dr. Wanda resides in Greenville, NC with her daughter, Anassa Thompson.

If you would like to contact Dr. Wanda, please email her at carrwdc@hotmail.com, via Facebook, Twitter (@lifelearner72), and find me on LinkedIn.

www.ingramcontent.com/pod-product-compliance
Lightning Source LLC
Chambersburg PA
CBHW061249040426
42444CB00010B/2313